This book, may not be reproduced, or stored, scanned, or photocopied, or used in any mechanical or electronic device, without a written copyright permission.

Bible references are taken from the King James Version

CONTENT PAGE

God's Handmaid 3
The Alternative Weapon................12
How to Activate the Anointing.....16
Overcoming Past Hurts............... ...21
Your Exit Strategy..................31
I will bring you out...................... 34
God's blueprint for the Woman......48
The emancipation of God's women.64
Repositioning to Reign..........93
For His Glory...…...............…....104
Joy in Sorrow..................…....107
Prayers..........................…....118
Testimonials....................….....128

God's Handmaid

'And Mary said, Behold the handmaid of the Lord; be it unto me according to thy word. And the angel departed from her.' Luke 1:38.

Mary was *fully* committed to her call, as the handmaid of The Lord. Everything she did, reflected this.

✿ *She thought* as the handmaid of The Lord. She took note of the declarations, from the angel. What she heard from the shepherds, she kept in her heart and pondered on them. *'And all they that heard it wondered at those things which were told them by the shepherds. But Mary kept all these things, and pondered them in her heart.' Luke 2:18, 19.* <u>**Mary was discreet**</u>**.** It's when God's word is internalised, that it becomes, a lamp unto your feet and a light unto your path. Psalm 119:105, Joshua 1:8.

✿ *She was humble.* She knew, the child she bore was the Son of God and laid no claim on Him. He came to serve His Father. Luke 8:19 - 21. She was only a conduit, a vessel in God's hands! ***She made no demands for recognition or reward as the mother of Jesus but submitted herself to His Lordship! Luke 2:49.*** She received the word of God with humility.

✿ **She surrendered to the will of the Lord, as His handmaid.** Mary's obedience to God's call contradicts Eve's disobedience in the Garden of Eden. Her acceptance was pivotal to her call. ***'Be it unto me according to Thy word.' Luke 1:38.*** The role of Mary in fulfilling Christ's Messiahship is unique, carrying in her womb, the Saviour, Jesus Christ, who is the fulfilment of eternity. Luke 1: 31.

There was no hesitation on her part, because she believed and trusted God, who had spoken concerning her. There are things you can only say and do through a deep conviction of the one you trust. She surrendered to God's will.

✿ **She spoke** as the handmaid of The Lord, from a place of faith. Mary praised God, even before the Child was born. *'....from henceforth all generations shall call me blessed.' Luke 1:48b.* Let us **consider her conversation.** She was not frivolous. She was a person of few words, not disposed to gossips nor idle words. Proverbs 10:19. *'And when they wanted wine, the mother of Jesus saith unto him, They have no wine. Jesus saith unto her, Woman, what have I to do with thee? mine hour is not yet come. His mother saith unto the servants, Whatsoever he saith unto you, do it. John 2:3 – 5.* She encouraged Jesus into His first miracle, ignoring His reluctance. *She reordered the divine sequence of time and positioned her Son for His first Miracle!* Heaven honoured her, though the time was not yet. John 2:4 - 11

<u>She did not say much, but she believed much</u>.

✿ **She denied herself, to become,** the handmaid of the Lord. She was crushed in spirit, as a mother, seeing her Son crucified, but she stood by Him. **'Now there stood by the cross of Jesus his mother, and his mother's sister, Mary the wife of Cleophas, MaryMagdalene.' John 19:25. Mary loved God more! She died to her maternal instincts so that every sinner who believed in Jesus, might live and not die;** that the redemption plan might be fulfilled. She ignored the rumours, and pointing of fingers, risked the possible loss of her betrothal, to Joseph, to put God First. She trusted God to do a thing never heard of before; a conception by the Holy Spirit. Luke 1:35. <u>How far can you trust God? How far, can your faith be stretched?</u> Her cousin Elizabeth, praised her faith in God. **Mary's journey to Bethlehem was her journey to her Calvary, where she would be stripped of any self-worth, or dignity, away from civilisation and comfort, where her first child would be birthed in a manger.** Luke 2:4, Micah 5:2, John 7:42. <u>Everyone has a cross to bear, a route to follow, to calvary, but the end is glorious. It is worth the journey!</u> **You have a defined role in God's kingdom, in the actualisation of God's plan on earth.** The call of God, on your life, requires self-denial. You cannot pursue unto the end in the flesh. Mary, surrendered, ***her parental rights as His earthly mother, because she knew from whence He came***. She knew He was God's gift to her. It's the price of a high calling! Letting go!

✲ ***She had a prophetic call, as the Lord's Handmaid***. In Mary's Magnificat, she prophesied of the coming of the Messiah, the liberation of the Jews. Luke 1:50 – 55. What a mighty Fortress is our God. Psalm 18:2, 71:3. She expresses the hope of those who look up to God, those who looked up to the coming of the Messiah. They shall be glad. Psalm 68:3, 104:34c. The expectations of the righteous shall not be cut off. Proverbs 23:18, 24:14c. But the proud shall be humbled, debased and the humble shall be exalted. They that put their trust in Him shall never be ashamed. Romans 10:11, Psalm 37:19. She declares the power of God, His sovereignty and the establishment of God's kingdom on earth. ***Mary had a revelation of the messiahship of Christ.***

'He hath shewed strength with his arm; he hath scattered the proud in the imagination of their hearts. He hath put down the mighty

from their seats, and exalted them of low degree.' Luke 1:51, 52

It re-echoes Hannah's prayer of thanksgiving.

<u>'The adversaries of the LORD shall be broken to pieces;</u> out of heaven shall he thunder upon them: the LORD shall judge the ends of the earth; and he shall give strength unto his king, and exalt the horn of his anointed.' 1 Samuel 2:10.

✽ **She was acknowledged. Despite the scepticism, which might have prompted Joseph, to consider the thought to put Mary, away. Matthew 1:19.** Elizabeth acknowledged her, as the mother of Christ, the Saviour, and received a further witness, as the baby in her womb, *leaped for joy!* Luke 1:42 – 45. There will be a witness of God's calling in your life in Jesus Name! Some, will acknowledge that you are called and chosen. *But beyond man's recognition and validation, you have an inner witness which validates you,* and that is God's presence, by the Holy Spirit. 2 Timothy 2:19a.

Although Mary had many outstanding qualities which enabled her to perform her role as a mother and a servant, the descent of the Holy Spirit upon her at the time of her conception might have **endowed her with the grace which characterised her ministry.**

'The Holy Ghost shall come upon thee, and the power of the Highest shall overshadow thee: therefore also that holy thing which shall be born of thee shall be called the Son of God.' Luke 1:35b.

✤ *Mary rearticulated the message, of the angel to her, Luke 1:28, in her own words, saying, 'For he hath regarded the low estate of his handmaiden.' Luke 1:48a.* God's Word is True. It was true that they will **Behold Him,** that will be born of her. Mark 9:15, John 1:14, Job 19:27. **You are how God perceives you to be. Acknowledge it, articulate it and believe it even when there are no physical signs or evidence. His word is Proof!** Don't seek for men's

approval. It takes time to win some hearts, some may never believe. *The only one to Believe is You!*

'And blessed is she that believed: for there shall be a performance of those things which were told her from the Lord.' Luke 1:45.

The Lord's Handmaid, is an Obedient Servant. *Mary's submission to God was integral to the accomplishment of God's plan for man's redemption; the encapsulation of eternity in the human.* God's vision for your life shall be birthed through the power of the Holy Spirit when in total submission to His will. *Every plan of God is supernaturally birthed.* Matthew 1:20, 21. Luke 1:37. Genesis 21:1, 2.

For unto you is born this day in the city of David a Saviour, which is Christ the Lord. And this shall be a sign unto you; Ye shall find the babe wrapped in swaddling clothes, lying in a manger. Luke 2:11, 12.

Self-validation. Mary knew who she was. Behold the handmaid of The Lord! She was comfortable with that and she declared it. She knew who she belonged to. God requires more handmaids in this end time May there be a great awakening.

The Alternative Weapon

The Alternative Weapon is the wise woman's weapon in warring through her battles. She overcomes the onslaughts of the wicked one with the Alternative Weapon. She is propelled by the anointing. She is led by God and navigates her way by God's spiritual GPS. She is mobilised with the Alternative Weapon.

God said to Zerubbabel, this mountain shall become a plain but not by your power or might but by My Spirit. God, by Himself, would level the mountains, impositions and oppositions. Zechariah 4:6, 7. **God**

might be saying, I have a better way of doing th for you! I will do this My Own Way, if you let Me! A better way of silencing the uproar. Our weapons of warfare are not carnal but mighty through God! That is the Alternative Weapon. IT IS THE ANOINTING, that breaks, dissolves the yoke, extinguishes the fire of the devourer, and strong holds dissipate That is GOD HIMSELF!

'And it shall come to pass in that day, that his burden shall be taken away from off thy shoulder, and his yoke from off thy neck, and the yoke shall be destroyed because of the anointing.' Isaiah 10:27.

Except the Lord, build the house, they that, labour, labour in vain. Psalm 127:1a. God is the Builder. Israel praised God's deliverance. *'If it had not been the LORD who was on our side, now may Israel say;' Psalm 124:1a. Victory is in God. Stand on the ROCK. Jesus is the Rock that never fails. Victory is on your side.*

✤ **The Wise woman picks her weapons discreetly. She weaponises the true Word of God, to her advantage. It is a sword of the spirit.** God's Word is the Alternative Weapon, when rightly applied. It will **do exploits, and become an armour in your hand.**

Leave your self-defence to God. He alone, knows how best to fight. Humans are not on the same plane or latitude with God, because He fights from Heaven. His ways are higher! As His thoughts. Isaiah 55:8. David said,

'God sent from above, he took me, and he drew me out of many waters.' Psalm 18:16.

- ✤ *Do not engage in battle with the same weapons as your opponent. You may lose in the battle.*
- ✤ You must pick up a higher weaponry, *an alternative weapon.* David rejected the ammunitions which were given to him because he had not tried nor proved their potency. **The Name of the Lord is the Alternative Weapon.** He said to Goliath

'...Thou comest to me with a sword, and with a spear, and with a shield: <u>but I come to thee in the</u>

name of the LORD of hosts, the God of the armies of Israel, whom thou hast defied.' 1 Samuel 17:45.

How to Activate the Anointing

You activate the Anointing, by setting up the right atmosphere for God to dwell in, to inhabit your home, fill and saturate every space with His presence, to war for you.

- ✿ *USE SOFT WORDS:* **Carefully choose your words.** In a tense atmosphere, words spoken carelessly, could aggravate the situation. *In a multitude of words there is sin. Proverbs 10:19a.*

But a soft answer turneth away wrath. Proverbs 15:1. Talk less. Be less vocal. Speak with grace. Soft words, quench the fire of the enemy, they melt away anger. Your kind words will confuse the enemy because **it was not the anticipated response**, so it dislodges your opponent, puts him off guard, <u>***and creates an atmosphere for God to fight on your behalf.***</u>

✤ *TAKE NO OFFENCE:* **Do not be easily provoked. 1 Corinthians 13:5.** When it is not fire for fire, you make room for God to step in. You will not invite God into a hostile environment? No. <u>**God will not fight your battles while you have your boxing gloves on.**</u> Be the first to drop them off, because there is joy set before you. Better days, days of His glory are ahead of you in Jesus Name! Jesus endured the cross, because of the Joy that was set before Him. Allow God to have the final say. He makes a way where there seems to be none.

✤ *FOLLOW PEACE:* Withhold not good from anyone who might have offended you. But follow peace with all. Continue on, with your daily obligations. Make delicious meals, feed the hungry, with good, overturn the counsel of the enemy. Your son, daughter, husband, wife, friend, enemy **are all categorised as all men**.

'Follow peace with all men, and holiness, <u>without which no man shall see the Lord</u>:' Hebrews 12:14

✻ *IGNORE:* Offences must come. Matthew 18:7. But learn to look the other way, to turn a blind eye. When you Cultivate this attitude, it will become a timely weapon to overcome every temptation. It might not be easy, but it will soon become a part of you naturally, once cultivated. There are higher things of eternal value to deliberate on. Let nothing else so consume your time and life span, except God. Some things are inconsequential. *Be less contentious. Walk away from arguments. It is not a sign of weakness, but of strength and wisdom.*

✻ *USE WISDOM:* The wisdom from above is first pure and peaceable because it leads towards peace. Its purpose, is to promote peace, honour and respect. Man's wisdom, on the contrary, is self-centred. Its purpose is **_for self-preservation._** Only for the benefit of self but leads towards self - aggravation, injury to self instead. **Craftiness *is not wisdom*.** It is cunningness. It leads to deception. That's its purpose, to produce a lie or falsehood. It is self-destructive. It does more harm than good.

✿ *LOVE*: Love never fails! Let nothing be done in vain glory, Love does no harm. but Love Covers and fulfils ALL the law. Because of YOUR LOVE FOR GOD, GO THE EXTRA MILE.

✿ *GIVE THANKS:* Don't lose your praise and thanksgiving. Don't lose your admiration for God and his goodness. In all things, give thanks! It will turn around for your good and for his glory!

✿ **FIX YOUR EYES ON THE GOAL:** Fix your heart on things of eternal value. Every other thing will pass away! Jim Reeves sang, *this world is not my home I'm just passing through. Some things just don't matter.*

Sometimes there are misappropriated expectations. Putting your expectations and loyalty in humans, and look to man for the fulfilment of your dreams and for validation. It is unfair to expect so much of anyone. No one can fulfil that. Only Jesus! Only Jesus satisfies. Isaiah 55:2.

God is FAITHFUL. May the Lord be your Alternative Weapon. May He equip you with His Anointing, and Power from His Presence. May He Strengthen you from heaven, erase every wrong doing, any hurt or bitterness. Nothing fashioned against you shall be able to prosper in Jesus Name. May He give to you, new wine, a new Vision. May God, enable you, to fulfil your dreams and passion, your heart's desire in Jesus Name. Amen.

Overcoming Past Hurts

God is leading you to a place of healing, and health, to a place of forgetfulness, of past hurts, and into a *glorious* new Beginning, by the revelation of His word. These are Simple steps to follow.

The truth is Powerful, it liberates. It is purposefully driven, and targeted. The word of God is *Immutable!* It fits into every aspect of life. *It is effective, when, what is taught or heard, is applied.* **'Ye shall know the truth and the truth shall make you free.' John 8:32.**

✳ ❁ **FORGET THE PAST:** *'Remember ye not the former things, neither consider the things of old. Behold, I will do a new thing;' Isaiah 43:18, 19a.*

God wants you to relinquish the heavy yokes you bear, to press forward to the mark of your high calling in Christ Jesus. The greatest healings take place within, in the mind. Some considered as rich and affluent in society, end their lives, not for lack of earthly necessities but because of unresolved issues within, which money could not eradicate. Sometimes appearances, are only a facade, a window dressing, the truth is within. There is no healing, without JESUS. Only JESUS, can make whole. *'For he maketh sore, and bindeth up: he woundeth, and his hands make whole.' Job 5:18.*

✳ ❁ ***DON'T DWELL ON PAST HURTS:*** Don't dwell on past hurts. Shrug them off. Lay aside every weight lest it weigh you down. Forget the past. Walk away from it. ***Whatever you dwell on, you reinforce.*** Do not dwell on the wrongs you have suffered. You will reinforce its power and grip on you. ***Magnify the good***

done. Don't glorify past, injuries and pain, but glorify Christ! The Bible gives a list of things to dwell on.

'Finally, brethren, whatsoever things are true, whatsoever things are honest, whatsoever things are just, whatsoever things are pure, whatsoever things are lovely, whatsoever things are of good report; if there be any virtue, and if there be any praise, think on these things.' Philippians 4:8.

✿ **Despise the pain:** Deny it the value you had put on it in the past.

Take away, from it, that place of importance in your life. Assign a zero value to it. Relegate it. When it becomes like nothing, then you are ready to embrace the new life. *Count it all dung.* When your past gains or losses become as nothing, you are ready for the New Life. Jesus *despised* the shame. Hebrews 12:2. Because joy was set before Him. There is joy set before you. Joy will come, in the morning, mourning may endure for a night.

✾**THEY DON'T BELONG TO YOU:** *You took on, unnecessary weight which do not belong to you.* Every handwriting of ordinance which was against you is nailed to the Cross. He took them on, instead of you. *'Blotting out the handwriting of ordinances that was against you, which was contrary to and took it out of the way, nailing it to his cross. Colossians 2:14.*

Watching my granddaughter's defence manoeuvres, at a netball pitch, she intercepts, the ball, as it heads towards her team. You have an unseen defender, intercepting every arrow of the enemy, heading towards you, on your pitch of life.

Every pain and injustice, you might have received, as a child of God, is to God, not to you. *It's not pers*onal. It's not about you. They
did not do it to you but to Him. Although, Saul, persecuted followers of Christ, putting some, in prison, others, he punished often, Acts 26:11, when Jesus,

appeared to Saul, on his way to further terrorise, the brethren, He asked, **'Saul, Saul, Why persecutest thou me? it is hard for thee to kick against the pricks. And I said, Who art thou, Lord? And he said, I am Jesus whom thou persecutest.' Acts 26:14c, 15.**

Even, so, whatsoever good, you have done for others, you have done unto the Lord. **'Verily I say unto you, Inasmuch as ye have done it unto one of the least of these my brethren, ye have done it unto me.' Matthew 25:40b.** God is faithful to recompense you.

The enemy's ultimate purpose, is to invalidate you. What you feel is only a fraction of what was intended, because they could not perform their enterprise. You are hid with Christ in God. **'For ye are dead, and your life is hid with Christ in God.' Colossians 3:3.**

✽ **THE PLACE OF FORGIVENESS** Once, was prompted by the Holy Spirit, when counselling a sister, with marital issues, to say, **to forgive her husband, as if it never happened**. God gives the grace.

Do not risk your salvation because of anger or bitterness because of anyone. Let nothing steal your joy nor your eternal inheritance. Nothing is worth it.

'Looking diligently lest any man fail of the grace of God; lest any <u>root of bitterness springing up trouble you, and thereby many be defiled;</u>' Hebrews 12:15.

Let the good done override the wrongs. *Even when it looks like there is no good, and you can't find any good done, <u>look through the eyes of Faith, you may find something good</u>. God has ways of stretching your faith.*

✿ GIVE THANKS

<u>You cannot live the rest of your life in the past.</u> You are a New Creation, and Old things are passed Away. Celebrate the crucifixion of Christ, and your salvation. Thank God for a new life. **Affirm your individuality and peculiarity. Recognise yourself as New.** Acknowledge that the hurt of past years is Wiped out completely; the stigma and every trace of Unforgiveness. This is a New Day

Abigail: The Wise Woman

Abigail was one of the Wise women recorded in scripture, who averted the plot by David, to exterminate her entire household. She was described as a beautiful and intelligent woman, a woman of good understanding. 1 Samuel 25:3.

It might have been an opportunity for her to expose the maladies of her husband, which she had to endure, but she preferred to do him no harm but good. **'She will do him good and not evil all the days of her life.'**

Proverbs 31:12. Her focus was on how to solve the problem, and diffuse the tension between her husband and David, the would be King. She intervened, and saved Nabal, and her entire family from total annihilation, although, he, was the sole perpetrator of his misfortune. The cruelty and wickedness of her husband, and unwise decisions, notwithstanding, she preserved a whole family. With motherly instincts and attributes, of a wise woman, she was persuaded to save and not to enhance destruction. Proverbs 14:1a. The wisdom of Abigail, was more than her words. She endured her husband's evil disposition and quietly interceded for him before David. She overcame, unannounced.

HER STRATEGY:

Gifts: She persuaded David, with gifts she sent to him, and his men, ahead of her. ***'Then Abigail made haste, and took two hundred loaves, and two bottles of wine, and five sheep ready dressed, and five measures of parched corn, and an hundred clusters of raisins, and two hundred cakes of figs, and laid them on asses. And she said unto her servants, Go on before me;'* 1 Samuel 25:18, 19a.**

'A man's gift maketh room for him, and bringeth him before great men.' Proverbs 18:16.

Her Position: She took a humble position, came down from her chariot and fell at his feet. 1 Samuel 25:24.

Her Words: It is when truth is conveyed to the benefit of the hearer, that it becomes profitable. She said to David, it will be for your best interest and benefit if you relent and not destroy a whole household. ***A hasty decision for a moment's gratification, can leave behind, dire consequences in a lifetime.*** Wisdom, looks beyond the present. It endures. She said to David,

'And it shall come to pass, when the LORD shall have done to my lord according to all the good that he hath spoken concerning thee, and shall have appointed thee ruler over Israel; That this shall be no grief unto thee, nor offence of heart unto my lord, either that thou hast shed blood causeless, or that my lord hath avenged himself: but when the LORD shall have dealt well with my lord, then remember thine handmaid. 1 Samuel 25:30, 31.

There ought to be something in your conversation which is to the benefit of the listener, even when, undeserved. That's how you convince your accuser, win the heart of your opponent, and overcome. **You overcome evil with good.** David said to Abigail, *'Blessed be the LORD God of Israel, which sent thee this day to meet me: And blessed be thy advice, and blessed be thou, which hast kept me this day from coming to shed blood, and from avenging myself with mine own hand. 1 Samuel 25:32, 33.*

Your Exit Strategy

'For by thee I have run through a troop; and by my God have I leaped over a wall.' Psalm 18:29.

✿ **You don't have to destroy it.**
Once, in a dream, searching for something to break open a door, in order to make a way, but the door opened on its own, without any force applied to it, and all I had to do, was walk through it! The door to your exit, to liberty, and freedom to serve God, will open on its own accord, and you will walk through it. Some walls and restrictions are not physical impediments but

spiritual structures of the enemy, to hinder you. The prison doors opened to Paul and Silas; the walls of Jericho fell down flat for the children of Israel; the last gate, the iron gate which led to the city, opened on its own accord to Peter; while the women were crying for who will roll away the stone from the tomb where JESUS was laid, they did not know that JESUS, was Risen, that the angel of the Lord had already, come down, and rolled away the stone and sat on it! Matthew 28:2. He Secured the tomb. You don't need to destroy or break a relationship, or marriage, to fulfil God's calling on your life. Despite what you might bear. **Wait on God and He will bring you out, when the time is Right. He will make a way for you to fulfil, your call and destiny. When He does it,** HE will be your defence. **He will back you up.** God sent angel Gabriel to Joseph in defence of Mary's call. Matthew 1:20.

✿ **Be graceful:** Say yes or no with grace! Show disapproval with grace.

Patience. God works with time. HE uses time. In His time, He makes all things, beautiful! There is a supernatural factor to all things .

Do it right: If you must, choose between God and man, obey God and trust HIM to handle the consequences for your obedience. The heart of the king is in His hands, and, like streams of water, He turns it, withersoever way, He will.

I will Bring You OUT

'I will open your graves, and cause you to come up out of your graves, and bring you into the land of Israel. And ye shall know that I am the LORD, when I have opened your graves, O my people, and brought you up out of your graves.' Ezekiel 37:12b, 13.

❋ You must **overcome within, to win overall.** Rise above the situation, confront your fears, **master your opponent and overcome,** whoever or whatever, overcome from within. *'After that ye have suffered a while, make you perfect, stablish, strengthen,* *settle you.'* **1 Peter 5:10b.** It's a training curve. Engage in positive confessions. ***It may not be right, but it is doing me some good for all things, are working together for my good.***

✣ Ignore. *You don't need to fight every battle.* **Some things just don't matter. So what**? are two words I learnt in my process. Take time to reflect and ask yourself, **Does it really matter? Has it any eternal consequential value?** If not leave it alone. ***Walk away from it. It might hurt, it might hurt your flesh, people may say things about you, wrongfully against you, you might suffer a loss, but leave it.*** Paul said 'But what things were gain to me, those I counted loss for Christ.' Philippians 3:7. Walk by faith and not by sight.

✣ **The endtime harvest**

In this end time, God is bringing out daughters of Zion, from heavy burdens; breaking yokes, that they might serve Him to their full capacity. That's what freedom is for. It's for His service. Israel was liberated from bondage in Egypt after four hundred years, to serve

God! Genesis 15:13. It was a fulfilment of His Covenant with Abraham.

That's what the '*let My people go' was about; that's why the colt that was tied, was released*, *it was for God's use, for Jesus to ride on into Jerusalem; that's what the anointing is for, it's for HIM, for His service. Don't sleep on it.* Make no excuses. It's for the kingdom and for the glory of God.

House keeping

'Giving no offence in any thing, that the ministry be not blamed: But in all things approving ourselves as the ministers of God, in much patience, in afflictions, in necessities, in distresses.' 2 Corinthians 6:3, 4.

❃ Some things are necessary. Some things may not be convenient, but give no room, for pride or frivolity. Be faithful in temporal obligations with the right attitude. keep home, Cook, put food out on the table. Be sure there is enough at home, that your family is well fed, home chores done, as convenient, as is possible. Wisdom is the principal thing. Proverbs 4:7.

❃ **It's a process. There is a maturing process and it is needful. Depending on the call, it may seem to take longer than you can bear;** *enduring others, and overlooking ingratitude.* JESUS learnt obedience by the things, which HE suffered. **Hebrews 5:8.** The stretching might seem unbearable but, be not weary. Do not give up. You will obtain your Reward, if you do not faint. *'And let us not be weary in well doing: for in due season, we shall reap, if we faint not.' Galatians 6:9.* **The taste of wine, is enhanced through its maturing process.**

❃ **Endurance, is acquired, through a process of time.** *It requires patience to articulate.* It is the capacity of something to last, or withstand the wear and tear of an unpleasant situation.

Praise HIM through it! When evil is spoken, of you, emanate good. Just thank Him, say, thank You JESUS. It might not make any spiritual or logical sense; it might seem like; you are the loser but trust God! Abide! Stand your ground, stand in faith in Christ alone, who will carry you through. After Having done all, STAND.

'Wherefore take unto you the whole armour of God, that ye may be able to withstand in the evil day, and having done all, to stand.' Ephesians 6:13.

Your Warfare is Accomplished

'Speak ye comfortably to Jerusalem, and cry unto her, that her warfare is accomplished, that her iniquity is pardoned: for she hath received of the LORD'S hand double for all her sins.' Isaiah 40:2.

'She hath done what she could'
JESUS said of the woman with the alabaster box of ointment, 'She hath done what she could.' It was that one act, which validated her. **It wasn't what she did but who she did it for, that qualified her for heaven's eternal compliment and ovation,** that anywhere the gospel is preached, her service will be remembered. <u>**All other works are good and have**</u>

their place, but serving JESUS, is the greatest and only enduring service. It is that which endures forever. You might have laboured long, and waited patiently, for God. Your service of love even when inconvenient is not in vain, whatever you lose for the sake of the Kingdom of God is profitable. It will turn into gain for you.

❀ Her critics

'But when his disciples saw it, they had indignation, saying, To what purpose is this waste? For this ointment might have been sold for much, and given to the poor.' Matthew 26: 8, 9.

Why trouble ye the woman, Jesus asked? Jesus is Always at your defence.

People murmured, criticised and condemned her. **But what they saw was not what the Saviour, saw in her.** Jesus came to save and not to condemn. . JESUS spoke up for her, as her Saviour, the Messiah, the *One* who Liberates from the oppressor.

Unfortunately, people try to *elect* who deserves God's love and mercy, and who does not. But God has the prerogative, not humans. ***God chooses, not man***. You may not be the choice of many, some may turn away, despise or malign you. ***You are chosen of the Lord!*** Jesus ignored, the multitude around Him, but called on Zachaeus a publican, a sinner, though disadvantaged, by his stature and occupation. He said to him, ***'Zacchaeus, make haste, and come down; for to day I must abide at thy house.' Luke 19:5.***

✿ Ignore your critics, but serve God! Do not be discouraged or intimidated. Since <u>**God has called you as a woman, serve HIM as you are, a woman . HE already knew who you were, before HE called you. Make no apologies for who you are. God created you and fashioned you as you**</u> are right from your mother's womb. God preordained you, and programmed you with a unique DNA to function in this capacity. If called as a wife, serve Him, as a mother, serve Him, as single, serve Him, just as you are. **Serve God! HE IS the only True and Living God. Let the whole world know the truth, by doing your bit. Amen** ☐

Talk To God

✿ ***Intimacy with God:*** How would it feel if you had a friend or family member whose phone line is always busy, engaged and you are unable to speak with him or her? Wouldn't you stop calling? If God calls or tries to connect with you, and you are preoccupied, too busy or unaware, would it be right? GOD'S phone line is always open. He is Never too busy to answer. HE has a special place in His heart for you. ***'Seek ye the LORD while he may be found, call ye upon him while he is near:' Isaiah 55:6. 'When thou saidst, Seek ye my face; my heart said unto thee, Thy face, LORD, will I seek.' Psalm 27:8.***

❈ *You are so unique that HE knows your voice!* HE cannot mistake your voice for someone else's because HE arranged your vocal cords. When you call, as you will today, GOD knows you are calling. The sheep knows her Shepherd's voice, but Her Shepherd also recognises the voice of His sheep. God is listening out for you! He longs to hear your voice. He knows you by name. Isaiah 43:1. You are inscribed in the palms of His Hands. *'Behold, I have graven thee upon the palms of my hands; thy walls are continually before me.' Isaiah 49:16.*
You are indelible!

❈ *God's workmanship*: You are not man-made; you are God's Handmade. You are not scripted, by human hands, but God's creation. You are *valuable* to HIM, of great value! Isaiah said, **'But now, O LORD, thou art our father; we are the clay, and thou our potter; and <u>we all are the work of thy hand</u>.' Isaiah 64:8.**
God's love is greater than any human faculties. It is invaluable, and unconditional.

When JESUS was on earth and till now, HE was moved by His love and compassion, not by the laws. **HE healed on a sabbath day, though it was unlawful to heal on the Sabbath day because there was a need. Luke 14:5. He is the Lord of the Sabbath.** He is the Lawgiver. **Nothing can exclude you from God's love and compassion.**

When the blind beggar called on JESUS for help, and HIS disciples rebuked him, there was something, in his voice which caught the attention of the Master and compelled Him to stop and HE called for him. He identified himself with Jesus, calling on Him, as the Son of David.

'And when he heard that it was Jesus of Nazareth, he began to cry out, and say, Jesus, thou Son of David, have mercy on me.' Mark 10:47

Others were like, spectators, but <u>only Bartimeus called out, and he received his sight.</u>

'Go thy way; thy faith hath made thee whole. And immediately he received his sight, and followed Jesus in the way.

✿ *Prayer:* It is estimated, that there are about six hundred and fifty prayers in the Bible and a consensus, that JESUS prayed about twenty-five different times. Prayer, is the only means of communicating with God, and receiving from God. ***Sometimes, prayer could be the only Lifeline!***

✿ *Reasons to pray:*
1. There are many reasons to pray. It is a command, an injunction. Pray without ceasing. 1 Thessalonians 5:17. Do it always. Don't stop praying. We are called into a life of prayer,
2. **His ears are open to our prayers:** God listens. *'This poor man cried and The Lord heard him and saved him out of all his troubles'.* Psalm 34:6.
3. God hears us and answers our prayers. *'For the eyes of the Lord are over the righteous, and his ears are open unto their prayers: but*

the face of the Lord is against them that do evil. 1 Peter 3:12

4. It is revelatory: It brings knowledge. *Call unto me, and I will answer thee, and shew thee great and mighty things, which thou knowest not. Jeremiah 33:3*

God's Blueprint for the Woman

'And the LORD God said, It is not good that the man should be alone; I will make him an help meet for him.' **Genesis 2: 18**

Helper: The Hebrew word in Genesis 2:18c, which describes Eve, as a helper, is **'Ezer'** which means to salvage, to recover, or give help when distraught. It is the same word in Hebrews 13:6b, the Lord our Helper, and in Psalm 46:1c, the Lord, a very present help in trouble.

The woman is sent from God, to assist humanity. To partner not only with Adam but with God. You are a gift from God. This is not a subservient role, as often presented. That wasn't God's original plan for the woman. God has not sent any woman on a mission into slavery or bondage nor to subjugate to society. This is pleasing men, not GOD. We are slaves to whom or what, we give allegiance to. Romans 6:16.

Mary, became, an *Ezer*, when the time of prophecy was fulfilled, because she accepted an *unscripted* role, even, as a virgin. **She chose to please God, defied her sceptics, put her marriage and credibility under scrutiny of men, for the sake of redemption of mankind.** [She partnered with God](). Eve was given to Adam not only for procreation, but to work with God. The woman is an intercessor, a procreator, an achiever, and helper, who receives from God, to give to man. **'And upon the handmaids in those days will I pour out my spirit.' Joel 2:29b.**

GOD never questioned nor doubted His plans and purpose for the woman. To work with God, is your first and primary role. You must be positioned, spiritually, emotionally, mentally, physically, to fulfil this role.

The Deception: Eve, was beguiled by the pretence of the serpent. She knew the truth but was deceived. She misjudged the intentions of the serpent, and thought it was for her good. **What she saw with her eyes, because it looked good, was a bait to destroy her and her position in God's blueprint for mankind.** The same method has persisted through generations, until now. The woman is deceived and deprived of her God given role, and lured into servitude. We sell ourselves, for nothing. Isaiah 52:3.

The Curse: 'And I will put enmity between thee and the woman, and between thy seed and her seed; it shall bruise thy head, and thou shalt bruise his heel. Unto the woman he said, I will greatly multiply thy sorrow and thy conception; in sorrow thou shalt bring forth children; <u>and thy desire shall be to thy husband, and he shall rule over thee.</u>' Genesis 3:15, 16.

Living under the curse and not the blessing, is a misconception which suits the world. An enslaved role, was a curse and consequence for the disobedience of Adam and Eve in the garden of Eden. **But the position Eve lost, was restored into Sarah. Sarai, became Sarah, the mother of nations, though she was past the age of child bearing, and brought forth Isaac, a type of Christ, as the promised seed of Abraham, the father of nations.** Two thousand years later, *not far from mount Moriah,* on the cross of Calvary, Jesus was crucified. He was made a curse for all who believe on Him. <u>**Christ took upon Him, your infirmities.**</u> Sister, you are no longer bound, to a curse. *God did not give up on the woman. HE chose, His Son, to be birthed, through a woman*, Mary; Mary, the mother of JESUS, our LORD and Saviour! Hallelujah! Amen!!!

The Troubling Silence

No abuse is godly! It is wrong and completely unscriptural and unethical. It does not reflect Christianity nor Christ's love. Cultural dispositions and religious influence on women are heartbreaking, that despite governmental initiatives, and women's awareness, in Christendom, statistics indicate an increase in the number of women living under emotional distress and abuse.

It is appalling that faith and religious obligations could be so misappropriated as a cloak for abuse, segregation and inequality. *Women are silenced and some live through unbelievable ordeals.*

The church, presents a misconception of the role of women, wives and the unmarried. **Cultural bias** lead to spiritual bondage. *Only the Words of God lead to freedom and justice. John 8:32. She that the Son sets free, is free indeed. John 8:36.*

Although women live through these ordeals, <u>what is most troubling is the SILENCE.</u> I saw an artist's impression of a perfect woman which was a female face without lips.

Women are not objects to be displayed or merchandise for sale, neither picture, for exhibits. This is probably why Queen Vashti refused to be paraded as the King's trophy, before the people, although it made room for Queen Esther. Esther 1:10 – 12. We have misplaced priorities and misjudged our callings as women.

The woman has of recent, taken up so many roles and for lack of the right word, it's called multitasking. Apart from being, the wife, and mother, she has taken up the leadership role in the home, in some cases, financially and spiritually. Not dwelling on where we are but where we ought to be, let us press forward, toward the prize of the high calling of God, in Christ Jesus.

Your Work is not in Vain

Congratulations on your exploits for the Kingdom. *It was an exoneration for women, when Paul, acknowledged the contributions of the female species in the spreading the gospel of Christ. 'I commend unto you Phebe our sister, which is a servant of the church which is at Cenchrea: That ye receive her in the Lord, <u>as becometh saints</u>, and that ye assist her in whatsoever business she hath need of you: for she hath been a succourer of many, and of myself also. Romans 16:1, 2.* <u>**Paul**</u>

acknowledged the help he received. Do not give up, nor give in, but be satisfied, knowing that your work is not in vain. The ONE who made the eyes, sees, the ONE who made the mouth, speaks. HE will speak on your behalf. Amen. Your service is unto God, not man. **There is only ONE who can say well done good and faithful servant enter into your rest.** *That's when your cross becomes a crown and losses turn into gain.* God remembered Noah on the floods! God will remember you too. Genesis 8:1.

❇ *Dorcas,* did not know, she was labouring towards her resurrection, and sowing towards that day. She had built up a repertoire of good works. She laboured with her hands and made garments; she gave from the work of her hands to many, and when her hour of need, came; a time for God's intervention, **her works, exonerated her.** The people presented her works to Peter, showing what she had done. **They pleaded with him, saying, that she was profitable to the kingdom, and to them, and deserved better.** *'And shewing the coats and garments which Dorcas made, while she was with them. But Peter put them all forth, and kneeled down, and prayed; and* *turning him to the body said, Tabitha, arise. And she opened her eyes: and when she saw Peter, she sat up.' Acts 9:39c, 40.*

Your works will speak for you! Seed time and harvest shall never cease. **It's to your credit. Paul said, *'Not because I desire a gift: but I desire fruit that may abound to your account.' Philippians 4: 17.*** Women, give in so many ways, in service, in humbleness, in church, home, in the community, as married and as single. It is all, to your own advantage. Some things you should know, lest you be wearied and faint in your mind.

The Call

❃ ***Obedience precedes fulfilment.*** It comes before the blessing! **Hearing from the Father comes with responsibilities. The greater part is obedience!** Fulfilment comes from being fully engaged in that which God has called you to.

The promise is actualised in obedience, by doing that, which you are called to. There is a part for human participation in the fulfilment of every prophecy, and by <u>doing it God's own way!</u>

✿ *Different Callings:* There are different callings but one Spirit, and faithfulness to the call on your life, is what qualifies for the 'Well done good and faithful servant.' It comes as an acknowledgement, of work accomplished.

The Proverbs 31 woman, excelled in home management, and functioned as an enterprise. Deborah flourished in legal and constitutional matters, as a judge, and a Prophetess. She had the word of God in her mouth. Esther at such a time, changed the course of history, and saved a whole nation, from the evil plot of Haman, to exterminate the Jews. Abigail, Mary the mother of JESUS, Rahab, Acquilla, each fulfilled, their distinguished role. Be faithful to that which God has called you to. **Only that, will be required of you!**

There are other women, children, nations, and people, waiting for you; to hear you, to rise up because of you. So, don't hold back the call. It is not for you, but for others out there. It is pertinent that you arise

❈ **You are first. In some instances, God revealed His plans first to the woman. Remember Samson's mother.** The angel of the Lord first appeared to Manoah's wife about the birth of Samson. Judges 13:3 – 6. When Manoah enquired of the Lord, the angel was sent back to his wife. Judges 13:8, 9.

Angel Gabriel was sent first to Mary, who was betrothed to Joseph, about His redemption plan. *'And in the sixth month the angel Gabriel was sent from God unto a city of Galilee, named Nazareth, To a virgin espoused to a man whose name was Joseph, of the house of David; and the virgin's name was Mary. And the angel came in unto her, and said, Hail, thou that art highly favoured, the Lord is with thee: blessed art thou among women." In Luke 1:26 - 28.*

Both instances were on the birth of a child. It's the woman, who naturally gives birth to a child. Zachariah was silenced by the angel, he became dumb after spoken to about the birth of John the Baptist, because he disbelieved. Luke 1:18 – 20. *There is more about the woman, and God knows. There is more, about you.*

The Bible records, several of God's encounter with women. He confided His plans to women. He still does.
==You are not behind. You are first with God.==

Jesus Christ

JESUS knew and understood HIS mission on earth. People had other opinions of HIM. They mischaracterised HIM. HIS divinity was questioned by religious institutions until HIS death on the cross. Herod mistook HIM for an earthly monarchy, as the King of the Jews and sought to kill HIM.

But JESUS knew who HE was and IS and will ever BE. HE said, I AM THE resurrection and The Life! I AM the way, the truth and the life! HE was seen as a revolutionist because HE confronted the traditionalists. When questioned about the woman caught in adultery according to the laws of Moses, HE said, if anyone of you is, without sin, cast the first stone. An eye for an eye, a tooth for a tooth was the laws given to Moses, but JESUS said, turn the other cheek; give your cloak, to anyone who asks, of you; go the extra mile. They accused Him of blasphemy, when He said, He was the Son of God. John 10:36. In John 6:48, He said, '**I AM THE BREAD OF LIFE.**'

❋ **Know whose you are. You are first and foremost the bride of Christ!** You are redeemed. You are HIS beloved. You are GOD'S delight, Hephzibah! You are the apple of HIS eyes.

You are good! He who finds a wife, finds a good thing and obtains favour from the Lord! You are man's passport to God's favour! That's who you are. You are equipped for the role and capable.

The Emancipation of God's women

In the world, there is a galvanisation of women, against female abuse; a shift in the atmosphere. Some societies, have seen, the first female formular 1 Driver. In other nations, women, were allowed, for the first time, to watch football matches and to drive a car. Delhi women were seen, learning to fight back against harassment and brutality.

Synchronisation

No automobile works well, when certain parts are out of synchronisation with other parts. It only functions properly, when all the parts are synchronised with each other. **It's when something is in the right position that it can Function. Functionality is relative to positioning.** The quality of being suited to serve a purpose well, depends on having the right person positioned in the right job. You need a licensed driver behind the wheels to ensure your safety on the road. ***May the Lord, situate you in the right place, with right relationships, to optimise your potentials and restore lost grounds to you.*** **YOU WILL OVERCOME WHAT OVERCAME YOU! IN JESUS NAME!!! AMEN.** *GOD will Reinstate you in Jesus Name! May He restore health to you! Remove any disorder, or misalignment. May any dysfunction, be undone, and form of disability, be healed in JESUS Name! Amen ☐ May God reposition you for the Kingdom in JESUS Name.*

Repositioning

A need for repositioning indicates a shift from an original or intended post. **GOD's repositioning of** women in this end time is about realigning with GOD's intended purpose for the woman, which is crucial to the move of GOD in this end time. *It is a part of the process which sets in motion the emancipation of GOD's kingdom on earth, towards, the second coming of Our LORD JESUS CHRIST.* It is to mobilise women to engage in the harvesting of souls into GOD's kingdom. Be occupied in this. **Women are communicators. This is what we do. Women are powerful influencers.** 1 Peter 3:1, says if any man obey not the word, they also may **without the word** be won by the **conversation of the wives. Not only by word of mouth.**

Society

Society has reprogrammed and rebranded the woman. We seem to have overlooked things of eternal value. **Our earthly passions overwhelm our heavenly calling, and vision. Our earthly commitments, sometimes override our zeal for the kingdom.**

Where your treasure is, there will your heart be also. Matthew 6:21.

Deborah

'And she said, I will surely go with thee: notwithstanding the journey that thou takest shall not be for thine honour; <u>for the LORD shall sell Sisera into the hand of a woman.</u> Judges 4:9.
Through you, the LORD will crush the enemy. The same spirit of Sisera, which enslaves, the children of God, will be crushed through the intercession of God's women in these end times.

The level of moral decadence in our communities, idolatry and spiritual decline can only be reversed and pulled down through women. *A mother, knows when the child is malnourished, or goes astray.* She feels any delinquencies either through her maternal instincts, or spiritual antenna, and goes on her knees, before God, to reclaim the soul of her child, through her intercessions. Barak knew the role of the woman in the liberation of the Jews and reconstruction of Israel.

People, are constantly bombarded by the pressures of this world. In some societies, according to a report of

December 9, 2009, people on the average, consume 100,000 words, or about 34 gigabytes of information, every day.

We need to localise our thoughts, to the Word of God, and *meditate on them, therein day and night. Joshua 1:8b.*

The word

Deborah had the word. She said to Barak, *'Hath not the LORD God of Israel commanded, saying, Go and draw toward mount Tabor, and take with thee ten thousand men of the children.' Judges 4:6,7.*
Positioning: She brought the word of GOD and **she initiated the move** into obedience. *'Up; for this is the day in which the LORD hath delivered Sisera into thine hand: is not the LORD gone out before thee?' Judges 4:14.* Mount tabor, was a place of settlement and battles, in Israel, in the lower regions of Galilee.

'Take your place! Mount up! For this is Your Day!

Israel had ten thousand men to battle, on foot, with Barak and Deborah accompanying them, but no chariots. They were men who were not trained for battle but *willingly offered themselves.*

Jabin's army, led by Sisera were war veterans, and well equipped for the battle. They had a **multitude of men, with *nine hundred chariots of iron.*** Therefore, speed was on their side. They had an advantage over Israel, or so it seemed.

They had the human advantage and could easily overtake Barak and his men, <u>But Israel had a tactical supernatural advantage because God was on their side.</u>

This battle, was for freedom, deliverance from captivity. It wasn't out of greed to enlarge a territory, but for the liberation of the people of God. The Bible says, that for ***twenty years, the children of Israel, were mightily oppressed and they cried unto the LORD; Judges 4:3.***

Wherever you maybe, and in whatever situation, the Lord says to tell you that the battle is already won. It was won on the cross of Calvary. Jesus paid the full price for your freedom, liberty, healing, and salvation with his precious blood. **<u>You could not pay the price. You could not heal yourself. You could not win in the war. But Christ did! This battle is the Lord's!</u>**

GOD FOUGHT FROM HEAVEN

'They fought from heaven; the stars in their courses fought against Sisera.' Judges 5:20.

God reconfigured, the stars and they fought for Israel. The stars might have changed their course, or dimmed their brightness, or beamed their lights against Jabin and his army to cause blindness. Whatever and however, **God will deploy His heavenly host to war for you in your hour of need.**

On foot, Israel overtook the chariots because God disenfranchised them. Sisera fled, he came off his iron chariot and fled but God did it. God sent him straight to his death. ***God has ways of bringing your battles to an end, no matter how hard, or <u>insidious</u> it might be. God will prove his word to you. That it is finished!***

Jael

There *was* peace between Jabin the king of Hazor and the house of Heber the Kenite, so Sisera misjudged her kindness, underestimated her capabilities. Being at peace with someone *doesn't make a collaborator, with them.* Jael made a choice. She chose to collaborate with God. **'Blessed above women shall Jael the wife of Heber the Kenite be, blessed shall she be above women in the tent.' Judges 5:24**

Life presents us with opportunities and *so* many choices. **You will discover that at those defining moments in life, there are choices to make; the choice you make determines, your destiny.**
David said, Thou wilt show me the path of life. Psalm 16:11. May the Lord guide your decisions in Jesus Name.

'Then Jael Heber's wife took a nail of the tent, and took an hammer in her hand, and went softly unto him, and smote the nail into his temples, and fastened it into the ground: for he was fast asleep and weary. So he died. Judges 4:21.
So God subdued on that day Jabin the king of Canaan before the children of Israel. Judges 4:23.

❃ **Women need each other**. What Deborah first initiated; Jael finished. **The prophecy of Deborah, that Sisera shall be sold into the hands of a woman**

was fulfilled in Jael. There are Deborahs and Jaels today! ***Only another woman will understand your pain because she has been through it too.*** A man may empathise but cannot feel nor understand the rigours of child birth or the emotions of a woman, except another woman who has been through it. It was another woman, Mary, a close relative, who stirred up the SEED in Elizabeth's womb. The Baby leaped with joy! **Let's take off the mask and look out for each other. We need each other.**

Deborah is a Hebrew word which means a bee. The lifespan of a worker bee ranges from six weeks (in the summer) to twenty weeks (in the winter). Most of her brief existence is spent gathering nectar to make honey.

According to Gee, "a bee in her lifetime makes only 1/12th of a teaspoon of honey" — a tiny fraction of the hundred pounds of honey that a typical colony needs to survive. *"The most remarkable thing isn't that she does the work; it's that she doesn't even do it for herself," she adds. A bee won't directly benefit from the honey she makes; instead, it will allow future generations to thrive after she is gone.*

This too, is how we can change the world, by not worrying about the size of our contributions but doing what we can, where we are.

All worker bees are female. They are essential to a colony and have many different roles. To name a few jobs worker bees do:

- Foragers: These bees leave the hive and bring back pollen and nectar.
- Nurses: These bees feed larvae, as well as tend to and support the queen.
- Temperature controllers: These bees ventilate the hive to ensure the honey temperature is right.
- Builders: These bees keep the hive clean as well as provide wax to construct the hive.
- Security guards: These bees defend the hive and keep out pests.

Gees Bees Honey Company

You are visionaries. This is the season to bring forth, and be occupied in the kingdom work. **You need to galvanise, for GOD's work, Revamp for His glory!**

May the Lord bless, and reconnect you to the vision in Jesus Name.

*'So let all thine enemies perish, O LORD:
but let them that love him be as the sun when he
goeth forth in his might.' Judges 5:31.*

The Price to Pay

Nothing comes free. There are always consequences to any decision made. You might lose everything but **CHOOSE CHRIST!** **D**on't settle for less. Even if it feels easier and more *palatable*, or convenient. You may receive all the accolades, *but Choose Christ. Don't go with the flow, Go with God!* <u>You may lose some friends but don't lose Christ.</u> <u>Don't lose your POST</u>. Whatever it takes, however long it may be,

Follow Christ, follow the vision to the END. THERE IS JOY SET BEFORE YOU, HIS JOY AWAITS YOU!

Deborah followed the vision. She had the ***'Did not God say?'*** She held on to the Word with tenacity. Like Deborah, you have the Word of God. **What did God say to you?** Hold on to the promise!

Others were afraid of Jabin's army. They were fractured and unable to face their enemies but she arose. She said, '***The inhabitants of the villages ceased, they ceased in Israel, until that I Deborah arose, that I arose a mother in Israel.*** ' *Judges 5:7*. **Take a Stand!** Your victory is not in bowing to the conventional but kneeling on bended knees to God.

What the world offers is temporal, momentary gains. What shall it profit a man if he gains the whole world but loses his or her soul. **Don't lose the commission!** You have, Jesus, but ***don't compromise the goal***. Don't **<u>relegate yourself</u>** to who or what you are not for temporal gains. That is **<u>cowardice.</u>**

GOD WILL WIPE AWAY YOUR TEARS

The Song of Deborah, in Judges chapter 5 is because of two women
1 Carried out the vision ✓
2. The other, made a choice ✓
3 THE LORD FOUGHT FROM HEAVEN ✓

God knows when you need the help most. He is timely, and sequential. He knows when to come in and overtake the enemy. *You need Heaven's assistance because it is Heaven's Vision.* **It is the Lord's Assignment!**

<u>YOU WILL NOT FIGHT THIS BATTLE ALONE</u>

Prophetess Anna

Anna, which means **hand** in Hebrew is introduced as the daughter of Phanuel of the tribe of Asher. Asher was Jacob's eighth son. Luke 2;36 – 38.

Apart from, Mary the mother of Jesus, who prophesied, and the four daughters of Phillip, the evangelist, **Anna** was the documented prophetess in the New Testament. She was still dutiful, and served the Lord, even in her older years. In her early years, Anna experienced the loss of her husband after only seven years of matrimony. It must have been devastating for her. She could have remarried but she committed herself fully to the Lord. The Bible says, that she lived in the temple and did not depart from the temple but served the Lord, day and night with fastings and prayers.

It is incredible how God works through our pains, to incubate something new, a closer walk with Him, a stronger desire for Him, drawing to the ==One who is always there==. Jehovah Shammah! When you need help, Jesus could be the only helper, Comforter, the closest friend. God is the husband to the widow, the Father to the fatherless. Jesus is the Lily in your valley, the Rose in the plains of your Sharon; the beauty amongst the thorns, the Bright and Morning Star. Jesus is your Dayspring.

Many acknowledge Anna as the first evangelist of Christ. The first to speak to the Jews about the Saviour as the Messiah, who was long awaited, the liberator, the one who would bring deliverance to those in captivity, to the Jews and all who believed in Him. The bible records Anna as a woman of great age. It's recorded that Anna was about eighty four years old when she met the Lord Jesus as a baby in the temple in Jerusalem, at the same time as Simeon did. Simeon blessed the child Jesus, and spoke to His mother but ***Anna spoke to the people.*** May the Lord incubate through you, a vision for the kingdom. *May you be a channel for His kingdom. Amen.*

Builders

The attributes of motherhood, are engrained in every female species, to bring forth, care, and nurture. Every woman, young or old is a mother, biologically or spiritually. Women are naturally, protectionists, in a good sense, of the word; Knowing how to protect and guard, their territories, against invaders, to secure, their homes. Women are keepers, they cover, and protect from harm. You cannot hurt a child, without a sharp reprimand, from the mother. Jesus spoke about Jerusalem, and said, **'How often would I have gathered thy children together, even as a hen gathereth her chickens under her wings, and ye would not.' Matthew 23:37**
Women are the perfectness of God's creation, because He took from what was already there, and

remade it more beautiful. You are created for God's glory. *Adam said, This is now bone of my bones, and flesh of my flesh: she shall be called Woman, Genesis 2:23. Paul said, 'we are members of his body, of his flesh, and of his bones.' Ephesians 5:30.*

You are God's creation, with a call, and an assignment from God.

✻ ***Feed the flock:*** You have fed, nurtured, children, siblings and even parents, spouses, friends and loved ones but now is the time, to feed with the truth, which is the Word of God. Teach a child the way that he should go, when he or she grows, shall not depart from it, and even if they do, the foundation would have been laid, which cannot be shaken. ***A child is a dependant.*** <u>***Anyone, young or old, who relies on you, for physical, emotional support, or spiritual guidance, is your child or spiritual child.***</u> Feed from a point of authority in the Word of God. It is only the Word of God on your lips that will save, and bring remedy to any situation, to orchestrate changes which will last, and endure. God cannot be mocked. That which a man soweth, shall he also reap. *You have fed with natural milk, now feed with spiritual milk. You gave daily bread, now give the Bread of life.*

Three times, Jesus probed Peter's love for Him in John 21: 15 – 17, and asked Peter, do you love Me?

'Simon Peter, Simon, son of Jonas, lovest thou me more than these? He saith unto him, Yea, Lord; thou knowest that I love thee. He saith unto him, Feed my lambs. He saith to him again the second time, Simon, son of Jonas, lovest thou me? He saith unto him, Yea, Lord; thou knowest that I love thee. He saith unto him, Feed my sheep.' John 21:15, 16.

A mother's love goes beyond providing physical sustenance, but also fortifies, providing, spiritual gains and comfort. You are a custodian of the truth, show them the way to God!

The Preservers

THE MOTHER OF MOSES

The Bible, says, that there arose a Pharaoh who did not know Joseph, and he wanted to destroy, the male Hebrew children, but he did not succeed. He said to the midwives, '***Every son that is born, ye shall cast into the river, and every daughter ye shall save alive.' Exodus 1:22.***

But there was a woman, Jochebed, the daughter of a Levi, who had a strategy, and she executed it.

And she made the basket of Moses, with bulrushes, which was intended to keep her child safe. Exodus 2:3. Bulrushes are plants which act as coagulants, to purify and filter water from toxic wastes and block wastes from filtering into the water. They were a seal, providing resistance to floods, to ***preserve*** the child. The Word of God is the spiritual bulrush which guards our hearts from spiritual contamination. The basket, was a 'Tevah' symbolic of the Ark that Noah, built. Genesis 6:22.

❂ The mother of Moses, positioned Moses's sister to keep an eye, on him, from a distance.
She did not know that the baby, she laid in a basket, by the brink of river Nile, would one day, be the deliverer. God saved a whole nation, through Moses. Moses was a Priest, a prophet, an intercessor, a servant of God. He overshowed Christ in many ways. As God brought Israel out from bondage to slavery in Egypt, through Moses, so also, are we delivered, from bondage to sin, into life eternal, through Jesus Christ. *'And as Moses lifted up the serpent in the wilderness, even so must the Son of*

man be lifted up: That whosoever believeth in him should not perish, but have eternal life.' John 3:14 Although, Moses grew up in Pharaoh's house, in Egypt, kept by Pharaoh's daughter. He knew, he was a Hebrew child. He knew his God, was the God of the Hebrews.

The wisdom of the Egyptian midwives, is incredible. They listened to Pharaoh, but feared God.  They did not, as the king of Egypt had commanded them, but saved the male Hebrew children alive, and preserved the lives of the Hebrew sons at birth. Exodus 1: 16 – 21. They told the King, that Hebrew women delivered quickly. ***'The Hebrew women are not as the Egyptian women; for they are lively, and are delivered ere the midwives come in unto them.' Exodus 1:19.*** This was a covering, and God blessed them.

✤ ***The true mother keeps alive.*** The true mother of the child, who stood before King Solomon, was willing to let go her child, to keep her son, alive. ***'Then spake the woman whose the living child was unto the*** *king, for her bowels yearned upon her son, and she said, O my lord, give her the living child, and in no wise slay it. 1 Kings 3:26a.*

✿ Mary Magdalene

When men turned away from the tomb, and the closest disciples of Jesus, abandoned the tomb because of its emptiness, and air of disappointment, ***it was a woman who stood to preserve the truth about Christ's Resurrection. She bore the testimony, that HE IS RISEN, one of the pivots of Christianity.***

Do not allow disappointment, nor discouragement cloud your mind that you lose the promise, and walk away; that you lose hope in the promise and in HIM, WHO PROMISED. <u>**Preserve the Church. Women are preservers and innovators. You know how to gather, to make something with little or nothing.**</u>

✿ ***The Spices:*** It was the women who took the spices to embalm, and preserve the Body of our Lord and Saviour Jesus Christ. ***While others, slept, they woke up!*** And very early in the morning the first day of the week, they came unto the sepulchre at the rising of the sun. **Sisters, daughters of Zion, Arise and Build,**

Preserve the Church, it is the Body of Christ. Embalmment is a word for preservation. Oil her, bring in the spices, put in your best, evangelise, help where help is required, unify, avoid gossips, volunteer if anyone asks. Do not disengage from the church or God's service.

✿ **THE WORD OF THE LORD TO HAGGAI**
'The glory of this latter house shall be greater than of the former, saith the LORD of hosts: and in this place will I give peace, saith the LORD of hosts.'
Haggai 2:9.

Christ, is the glory of the latter House. He is the soon coming KING. Arise and build!

Who is Called?

When GOD makes a move, HE uses women as HIS instruments. He **uses the despised, and the unlikely.** Children of youth, are like arrows in the hands of a mighty man, even so are women in God's Hands. Psalm 127:4. Every believer is called. Come as you are, married, or single, young, or old. ***The walls of Jericho fell down flat because a woman was strategically positioned to facilitate it.***

The Bible records that **her house *was* upon the town wall, and she dwelt upon the wall**. **A fortification for the city from invaders. It was a point of entry** into Jericho. Rahab, was at a vantage point, and could see who was coming in and who was going out. Others might have thought she was so positioned, to profit her enterprise, as a harlot. But it was for God's kingdom purpose.

❋ **Her wisdom, was impeccable.** God knew her. **Others focused on her weakness but she focused on God!** *'And the woman took the two men, and hid them, and said thus, There came men unto me, but I wist not whence they were: And it came to pass about the time of shutting of the gate, when it was dark, that the men went out: whither the men went I wot not: pursue after them quickly; for ye shall overtake them.' Joshua 2:4, 5.*

Her efforts to save, were remarkable. *'But she had brought them up to the roof of the house, and hid them with the stalks of flax, which she had laid in order upon the roof.' Joshua 2:6.*

❋ **She had great faith in God. Her confidence, was in the GOD of Israel.** She spoke prophetically about Israel occupation of the land and God's promise which was later revealed to Joshua. ***Joshua 6:2. 'And she said unto the men, I know that <u>the LORD hath given you the land,</u> and that your terror is fallen upon us, and that all the inhabitants of the land faint because of you.' Joshua 2:9.***

✿ She risked her safety, to save the spies. It was preordained, that she would be of the mother of Boaz, the father of Obed, father of Jesse, who bore, David, ancestors of Jesus Christ, the Son of David. Her missteps could not change this, men's opinions could not.

'And the men pursued after them the way to Jordan unto the fords: and as soon as they which pursued after them were gone out, they shut the gate.' Joshua 2:7.

Although God had promised Joshua Jericho, the King, and the mighty men, Rahab was part of the plan to actualise it. She took the risk, hid the spies to aid to accomplish God's plan.

The role of Rahab in GOD's plan for Israel, could not be disproved. ***GOD needs the Rahabs. Women,*** *without any theological background, but have a great love for the LORD, who will be the watchmen and women, to stay on the mountain top to intercede for the church.*

How can a woman be repositioned for the end time mission, to take her rightful place? Learn to prioritise. Change your passions and desires. Some things may be necessary but we need to prioritise! Put GOD First!

The man, may be the head of the home, but stability is hinged on the woman, often referred to, as the neck, or the weaker vessel. **GOD hides Strength in things we despise or see as humble. It takes *strength to carry, and to bring forth.* It requires some emotional ability, to withstand pain. You are GOD's instrument and weapon of war. God needs you today.**

Repositioning to Reign with Christ

Repositioning of women, is about coming back to GOD, to your first LOVE! *There must be a spiritual and sometimes geographical shift, in order to gain access into your inheritance. We need regenerated minds, to realign with God's Word. It requires a deliberate effort on your part. It requires recalibration of some aspects of life.*

How to reposition
1. *Through knowing who you are (based on the word of God)*
2. *Through Acceptance. Receiving the word as the truth.*
3. *Through Agreeing with God. Amos 3:3.*
4. *Through Application. By living out the word.*

Why reposition?
1. *To occupy.*
2. *That you might be who you were made to be.*
3. *For the glory of God*

When God said to Moses to move forward after the apostasy of Israel, Moses asked Israel to reposition themselves. 'Who is on the Lord's side? let him come unto me.' Exodus 32:26b.

TRUE SELF PERCEPTION

To know yourself, to have a true self-perception will lead to right choices, and re – evaluation of self. Making the right choices, will alter your personal perspective on life and propel you into your destiny.

SELF-IDENTIFICATION

You are God's creation. Created by God in God's own image and likeness. Genesis 1:27. Though formed, from man, Genesis 2:21 – 24. You are God's creation, not man's creation. Man was created by God. Man cannot create or reproduce itself only God creates. <u>*He made them male and female.*</u> *Mark 10:6.* **There is neither Jew nor Greek, there is neither bond nor free, there is neither male nor female: for ye are all one in Christ Jesus. Galatians 3:28.**

- *You are not subordinate to man, but a partner and helper.*

GOD HAS A PLACE FOR YOU.

The First Lady role was first created by God, Himself, when He formed Eve. Adam's assignment had to be accomplished with the help of Eve. When God called Abraham. 'As for me, behold, my covenant is with thee, and thou shalt be a father of many nations.' Genesis 17:4. God created a role for his wife Sarah. He **gave Sarah an appointment, a portfolio** .

'And God said unto Abraham, <u>As for Sarai thy wife</u>, thou shalt not call her name Sarai, but Sarah *shall* her name *be*. And I will bless her, and give thee a son also of her: yea, **I will bless her, and** <u>*she shall be a mother of nations; kings of people shall be of her.* *Genesis 17:15, 16.*</u>

Disabuse your minds of the notion, unfortunately held by some in Christendom that only the man is called. <u>*God never said so*</u>.

ZION

Nothing reproduces its kind without the female. The womb is in the woman. **'For as soon as Zion travailed, she brought forth her children.'** Isaiah 66:8c. The earth  cannot bring forth without you! ***It's the woman, that feels the pain which propels the birthing process. This is the time to travail!***

'Before she travailed, she brought forth; before her pain came, she was delivered of a man child. Who hath heard such a thing? who hath seen such things? Shall the earth be made to bring forth in one day? *or* shall a nation be born at once? for as soon as Zion travailed, she brought forth her children. Shall I bring to the birth, and not cause to bring forth? saith the LORD: shall I cause to bring forth, and shut *the womb*? saith thy God.' Isaiah 66:7 - 9.

Isaiah 66, verse 11, takes cognisance of the female attributes. **'That ye may suck, and be satisfied with the breasts of her consolations; that ye may milk out, and be delighted with the abundance of her glory.'** *Galatians 4:26, says,* ***'But Jerusalem which is above is free, which is the mother of us all.'***
<u>God is characterised by both Male and Female functionalities and attributes.</u> *'As one whom his mother comforteth, so will I comfort you; and ye shall be comforted in Jerusalem.'* He comforts like a mother!

You are not a backdrop or window dressing. **You are the Zion of God, the daughter of Zion.** *Life is in you and comes through you. You are Called, Blessed, Anointed and hand-picked by the Most High God. You are most Blessed!*

David said to the Lord, *'For thou hast possessed my reins: thou hast covered me in my mother's womb.'*

'My substance was not hid from thee, when I was made in secret, and curiously wrought (shaped, formed, made) in the lowest parts of the earth.' Psalm 139:13 - 15.

He describes his mother's womb as the lowest parts of the earth. He was made in secret in his mother's womb!

Every woman, biologically, or spiritually, makes a man. By caring and nurturing, and travailing! **T**he child is **insulated** in the mother's womb.

Sisters, the emancipation of women, is about <u>partnering with God to birth Zion</u>! 'For we know that the whole creation groaneth and travaileth in pain together until now.' Romans 8:22. **Read verse 19.**

Every vision is susceptible to the attacks of the enemy, in its infancy. It's in its fragility that the enemy seeks to abort God's plan, either in the womb, in the birthing process, or early years. Matthew 2:13. God hides the vision for the right time; the Appointed Time. Romans 9:9. or its Due Season. Galatians 6:9, though often misjudged as a delay.

You are highly favoured. (Luke 1:28)

You are blessed among women. (Luke 1:42)

You are a royal diadem in the hand of thy God. (Isaiah 62:3)

You are filled with the Spirit of The Lord. (Joel 2:28,29)

You have found favour with God. (Luke 1:30)

You shall be called Hephzibah, and thy land Beulah: for the LORD delights in you. (He has taken recognition of you). (Isaiah 62:4b)

You shall also be a crown of glory in the hand of the LORD. (Isaiah 62:3)

Behold, your salvation cometh. *(Isaiah 62:11)*

You shall no more be termed Forsaken!

You are formidable!

Eternity

There is hope, for a reunion with loved ones, who have departed. Life is in seasons but through each season, the Word of God brings comfort, and hope.

'But I would not have you to be ignorant, brethren, concerning them which are asleep, that ye sorrow not, even as others which have no hope. For if we believe that Jesus died and rose again, <u>even so them also which sleep in Jesus will God bring with him.</u>' **1 Thessalonians 4:13, 14.**

The Word of God becomes our anchor; the light which shines in our dark *moments*, to lead and guide through each season.

'Thy word is a lamp unto my feet, and a light unto my path.' **Psalm 119:105.**

Be assured of God's Divine Presence. *'I will never leave you nor forsake you. Hebrews 13:5c.* God is always there! JEHOVAH SHAMMAH!

'When thou passest through the waters, I will be with thee; and through the rivers, they shall not overflow thee: when thou walkest through the fire, thou shalt not be burned; neither shall the flame kindle upon thee.' Isaiah 43:2.

'Yea, though I walk through the valley of the shadow of death, I will fear no evil: for thou art with me;' Psalm 23:4a.

Through the vicissitudes of life; over the mountains and in the valleys, God is forever constant. Though death comes, still, we shall behold Him, face to face. Job declared his faith in God '***And though after my skin worms destroy this body, yet in my flesh shall I see God:' Job 19:26.***

Jesus said to Martha, ***'I am the resurrection, and the life: He that believeth in Me, though he were dead, yet shall he live:' John 11:25b.***

The believer never dies, as we perceive it. Life is unending. *'And whosoever liveth and believeth in Me shall never die. Believest thou this? John 11:26. 'For He is not a God of the dead, but of the living: for all live unto him.' Luke 20:38.*
They are alive which die in Christ!

There is a word for each season and chapter of your life. *May you discover the Word for this season, the wisdom, for each day, and the grace to live it!*

For His Glory

Death is not, the conquest of the enemy, but a sign of great repose in God's will. **'O death, where is thy sting? O grave, where is thy victory?'** 1 Corinthians 15:55.

The unexpected loss of a loved one, is not a sign of God's absence. Martha, interrogated Jesus, on His delayed response to her brother's indisposition. **'If you were here, my brother would not have died.'**

Whatever God *permits*, will be for His glory at the end. God's unseen strategies are beyond human computation. He utilises the schemes of the enemy, for the furtherance of His purposes, to accomplish His divine Will on earth. All things, whether good or bad, shall become advantageous to your divine purpose, in life, that the scriptures might be fulfilled!

'And we know that all things work together for good to them that love God, to them who are the called according to his purpose.' Romans 8:28.

His works are irreplaceable, and irrevocable. Trust His ingenuity! **His ways are composite!**

'For my thoughts are not your thoughts, neither are your ways my ways, saith the LORD. For as the heavens are higher than the earth, so are my ways higher than your ways, and my thoughts than your thoughts.' Isaiah 55:8, 9.

Joseph said to his brethren, *'But as for you, ye thought evil against me; but God meant it unto good, to bring to pass, as it is this day, to save much people alive.' Genesis 50:20.*

How often we prejudge, and miscalculate God's intentions. We equate victory with gains without losses and success with accumulation of wealth. Sometimes, great victories are *intangible*; *incalculable*, and not easily perceived.

Although the disciples, had been forewarned, yet it had no logical meaning that healing had to come through death, that a corn ☐ of wheat had to die, to bring forth fruit. So, when Jesus tried to pass this logarithm on to His disciples, it was *vehemently rejected by Peter.* You know, with logarithms, you increase the base by multiplication; which is a mathematical principle. It was unusual to **Increase** by **Decrease**. Peter could not grasp the truth. Far be it from You, Peter, said to His Master, Jesus, about His betrayal and Crucifixion. Get thee behind Me, were the Words of Jesus to Peter. Thou savourest not the things that be of God but the things that be of men. Mark 8:31 - 33.

Joy in Sorrow

'Weeping may endure for a night, but joy cometh in the morning.' Psalm 30:5c.

Life is transitory and sometimes soon interrupted indiscriminately. The source of our hope and joy is life eternal, knowing that though this life perishes, we shall see our loved ones again! **'For the Lord himself shall descend from heaven with a shout, with the voice of the archangel, and with the trump of God: and the dead in Christ shall rise first:' 1 Thessalonians**

4:16. May the Lord bless, comfort and strengthen you.

'And ye now therefore have sorrow: but I will see you again, and your heart shall rejoice, and your joy no man taketh from you.' John 16:22.
Whatever life offers, Rejoice. *Don't lose your joy!*
The enemy is a liar, he comes to steal, to kill, to deprive you of attaining your goal in life, but *joy empowers* you.

Be of good cheer for I have overcome the world. John 16:33c. Christ has overcome for you. He conquered sin and death.

'For this purpose the Son of God was manifested, that he might destroy the works of the devil.' 1 John 3:8c.

Be optimistic. Be of a cheerful disposition, because the battle is already fought and won. It is not implied, that there are no battles, but that you might <u>know, your position; where you stand in the face of the battle.</u> Live from the position of strength; war, from a place of victory, knowing that Jesus Christ has already given you the Victory.

Have the mindset of an overcomer! *'Nay, in all these things we are more than conquerors through him that loved us.' Romans 8:37.*

'Rejoice in the Lord alway: and again I say, Rejoice.' Philippians 4:4.

In all things, give thanks. 1 Thessalonians 5:18.
'Verily, verily, I say unto you, That ye shall weep and lament, but the world shall rejoice: and ye shall be sorrowful, <u>but your sorrow shall be turned into joy.</u>' John 16:20.

LET NOTHING STEAL YOUR JOY! Praise God in the midst of the storm. Joy is not the absence of conflict, but the evidence of *relentless* faith in God.

When the disciples, in the midst of the storm, thought Jesus was uncaring, **'Master, carest thou not that we perish?' Mark 4:38c.**

But **Jesus Cares!** He arose and calmed the storm. *'And he arose, and rebuked the wind, and said unto the sea, Peace, be still. And the wind ceased, and there was a great calm.' Mark 4:39.*

Jesus is in this boat with you. May His peace override any storm in your life. HE is the Prince of Peace; Jehovah Shalom!

Hope in God

'Why art thou cast down, O my soul? and why art thou disquieted within me? hope in God: for I shall yet praise him, who is the health of my countenance, and my God.' Psalm 43:5. When hope is lost, faith diminishes.

Hope deferred makes the heart sick. It is humanly expected that what is hoped for, will be achieved. But we cannot live by sight and by faith concurrently. **'For**

we walk by faith, not by sight. 2 Corinthians 5:7. *'The just shall live by faith.' Romans 1:17c.* Faith in an Unseen God, faith for things not yet concretised, but hoped for. Our faith, is in the God, who does the impossible, calling things that be not as though they were; ***things non-existent into existence,*** declaring the end from the beginning. **Don't give up on God!**

You might have, prayed, fasted, and at a point of *helplessness*, but whatever the circumstantial evidence, might be, it is inconsequential in God's Divine blueprint for your life. **God will do, what He said He will Do!** May God, lead you to a place of hope and healing. A place of *pain* is the place for *healing*, the place of *death* is the place for <u>resurrection</u> **on the flip side**.

Although the tomb where Jesus was laid, was empty, Mary Magdalene, stood still, by the tomb. Although the disciples, had dispersed, she stood. John 20:10, 11. She looked beyond the *emptiness* and became the first to witness the resurrection; the Resurrected Christ. <u>*Look beyond the physical!*</u>

Looking unto Jesus the author and finisher of our faith; Hebrews 12:2a.

<u>Delayed promises and unforeseeable circumstances, do not diminish the efficacy of the Word of God</u>. God's Word is impermeable, indelible. Has He not spoken; shall He not make it good?

'For ever, O LORD, thy word is settled in heaven.' Psalm 119:89

Your expectations shall not be cut off. It's the expectations of the *righteous*, which *endures, recuperates*, and *accomplishes!* It shall not be taken away. **Your expectations lay a demand on God, and propel a Response from Him. It fuels your hope and hope generates faith.** *Faith is the evidence of things hoped for. Hebrews 11:1a.* Hope is like a <u>reservoir!</u> Be hopeful. **'Christ in you, the hope of glory.' Colossians 1:27.**

Faith is integral to your earthly existence. Salvation is received through Faith in God. Have faith in God, *even now*. Faith is your **divine Currency**, which Receives from God. ==Faith recalibrates, it turns situations around.== It is the pathway to God.

For, without faith, it is impossible to please God. Hebrews 11:6. Faith is like a conveyor belt *connecting* to God's heart and His provision. Faith rejoices in the storm. **Faith makes whole!** Matthew 9:22.

The Prayers of JESUS

'Father, I thank thee that thou hast heard me. And I knew that thou hearest me always:' John 11:41c, 42a.

'O my Father, if this cup may not pass away from me, except I drink it, thy will be done.' Matthew 26:42c.

'Father, forgive them; for they know not what they do.' Luke 23:34b.

'I thank thee, O Father, Lord of heaven and earth, that thou hast hid these things from the wise and prudent, and hast revealed them unto babes: even so, Father; for so it seemed good in thy sight.' Luke 10:21.

'Father, the hour is come; glorify thy Son, that thy Son also may glorify thee:'

'I pray for them: I pray not for the world, but for them which thou hast given me; for they are thine. Holy Father, keep through thine own name those whom thou hast given me, that they may be one, as we are.' John 17:9, 11.

'I pray not that thou shouldest take them out of the world, but that thou shouldest keep them from the evil.' John 17:15

'Our Father which art in heaven, Hallowed be thy name. Thy kingdom come.

Thy will be done, as in heaven, so in earth.

Give us day by day our daily bread.

And forgive us our sins; for we also forgive every one that is indebted to us. And lead us not into temptation; but deliver us from evil. Luke 11:2 – 4.

'Father, into Your hands I commit My spirit.' Luke 23:46b. NKJV.

Prayers for when divorced, or Separated

IT IS WRITTEN

'A bruised reed shall he not break, and the smoking flax shall he not quench: he shall bring forth judgement unto truth.' Isaiah 42:3.

'Behold the LORD hath proclaimed unto the end of the world, Say ye to the daughter of Zion, Behold thy salvation cometh; behold, his reward is with him, and his work before him.' Isaiah 62:11.

MY PRAYER

Lord, You are the Restorer.

You restore broken lives and broken dreams.

You bring recovery to the afflicted,

Hope to the despondent

Life to the desolate.

You are the Lily in the valley, the Rose in the plains of Sharon.

Your Hands make whole.

My Father, my hope is in Your unfailing love.

My trust is in Your Divine Constancy.

Rebuild my life.

Put the broken pieces of my life together and heal my wounded heart.

A smoking flax, You will not quench,
Whoever comes to You, You will in no wise cast out.
Please heal my brokenness and restore me.
Forgive my sins and any misdemeanours on my part.
Give to me a brand-new life
I pray in Jesus Name.

MY DECREES

By God's healing power, I forget those things which are behind
I consider them not
I do not dwell on them
I move forward to the things which are before me

God will navigate my path and lead me into my divine destiny

He makes my crooked places straight before me, and rough places smooth.

He will reorder my steps

I disengage myself from every attachment to past failings and disappointments

My mountains have become a way

I have lost nothing

I am recovered,

I am restored, I am vindicated.

God has restored to me, the years that the locust hath eaten, the cankerworm, and the caterpillar, and the palmerworm. Amen.

For I know that all things work together for good to them that love God, to them who are the called according to His purpose.

Every bitterness, anger and resentment are washed away by the anointing of His presence.

THANKSGIVING

Thank You Lord for You have heard my prayers. I receive Victory over my accusers in the Name of Jesus. I receive Your healing. David said, 'When my father and my mother forsake me, then the LORD will take me up.' Psalm 27:10.

There is therefore now no condemnation to them which are in Christ Jesus, who walk not after the flesh, but after the Spirit. Amen.

Prayers for the bereaved, when loved ones are no longer there.

IT IS WRITTEN

'For his anger *endureth but* a moment; in his favour *is* life: weeping may endure for a night, but joy *cometh* in the morning.' Psalm 30:5.

'To appoint unto them that mourn in Zion, to give unto them beauty for ashes, the oil of joy for mourning, the garment of praise for the spirit of heaviness; that they might be called trees of righteousness, the planting of the LORD, that he might be glorified.' Isaiah 61:3.

MY PRAYER

Lord, please fill this vacuum in my life with Your presence.

Carry me through this valley.

Open my eyes to Your unfailing love.

Fill my heart with your peace.

Reside in me Holy Spirit.

Help me to receive Your unfathomable love for me.

Holy Spirit, You are the Great Comforter. Be my Comforter.

Wipe away my tears Lord,

Turn my mourning into dancing and my sorrow into joy according to Your Word in Jesus Name. Amen.

Holy Spirit, You are welcome into my life, You are welcome in this place. Have Your Way.

Please bring Restoration and healing to my body, soul and spirit in Jesus Name.

MY DECREES

I am whole

I am refreshed by the refreshing of the Living waters

I receive beauty instead of ashes

The oil of joy instead of mourning,

I am no longer desolate nor forsaken

I am called by a new name; Hephzibah

I am God's delight

I shall be sought after

According to the revelations of Isaiah the Prophet

My empty spaces are filled

And I shall say in my heart,

Where have these come from?

Who hath brought forth these?

Behold I was left alone; these, where had they been?

THANKSGIVING

Lord I receive Your comfort. My hope is in Your Word, that we shall meet with our loved ones again, for all who die in Christ shall be resurrected with Him on the last day. Jesus said, that whoever believes in Him, though he (she) were dead, yet shall he (she) live: John

11:25. Thank You Lord for this Blessed Assurance. Amen.

Jesus is the Resurrection and the Life

Testimonials

 My name is Rhona Marshall. **God called me to do things I did not know I was capable of doing.** I failed at everything when I was young. Failed my eleven plus, emigrated to Australia in 1961 no "O or A" levels. I'm very practical and a born organiser. Also dyslexic, hardly read apart from the Bible. I was a landlady of two pubs with my husband, then he fell in love with another lady, and we got divorced. Three years later in 1987 I became a Christian and my life changed 100%

He called me to Uganda in 1991. He told me to wait and said "stability of your children is most important" God blessed me in 1995 when Sarah was 24 and Emma 21. He opened every door, and he gave me a heart for the needs out there and blessed and blessed me. Yes, there have been huge challenges 'BUT GOD' has sustained everything and I'm so grateful for what He chose me to do in Uganda for him. Some of the children, who are now in their late 30's early 40's are around the world doing amazing jobs. I feel very, very blessed.

In 1996 we set up the **Christian Relief Uganda**. We had the 27th Anniversary in Uganda on Aug 12th 2023. So many lives have been changed . **David Young, who ran "Children for Christ" came with us in 2005.** *Hundreds of children came to know the Lord as their Saviour.*

In **2008 I was blessed with an MBE. The Queen gave me my award which I couldn't have had if all the CRU Committee**  **hadn't been alongside me and doing their bit.**

In 2012 March 5th Rotary gave me a **Paul Harris Fellow Award and** Senior Fellow of the Noble Communion & Holy Apostolic Order of Saint Hadrian of Canterbury, award in Southwark Cathedral, in 2013. I Set up Macclesfield Pioneering Women with three other ladies, in **2014**.

God called me to write a book in 2012, ' ***THE CALL, THE COST, THE CHOICE.*** ' He gave me every step as I went along.

It hasn't all been plain sailing; 2014: a metal knee, 2019: I had breast cancer, Operation on my foot in 2021: a suspected heart attack. But God has always been with me and got me through. ***It has made me realise just how much the Lord has done through being available and surrendering*** to the Him on **May 14th 1987**. There is always **a team of people** that God sends me to help when I do things, this certainly isn't all me.

On the night I became a Christian the Lord said to me "You think you've lived an exciting life so far, just wait till you see what I've got in store for you"

Email: Rhona_cru@talktalk.net

Mobile: 07968 168 949 or 01625 618319

My name is Charmain Sangster
When Mercy Says NO!

I've been diagnosed with cancer twice. First, with stage 2 breast cancer in November 2009, which consists of gruelling treatments. At that time, I was also in an abusive marriage. At the end of the 10 years of treatment for breast cancer (which was 2020), I was diagnosed with two different cancer (not secondary) and had a stroke during a double surgery over six hours. Still on the journey of recovery with the help of God.

I'm currently involved with the NHS, because of my journey. I want to share my story to bring awareness to living with and life after cancer and the **love and power of JESUS!** My goal is to help save lives and educate others to be aware/knowledgeable of changes in their bodies.

Before and during those challenging times, my faith in Jesus Christ played a vital and crucial role in my recovery. When I look back, I see, that God was preparing me for what was ahead, before I got diagnosed, by giving me scriptures and speaking to me in various ways, through these verses of scriptures, but I had no clue of what was in the bible * Zechariah 2:5 NIV. **'And I myself will be a wall of fire around it,' declares the Lord, 'and I will be its glory within.'** The Holy Spirit dropped this in my spirit two days before I was admitted in hospital with blood cloths in my lungs during chemotherapy where I was exposed to MRSA (there's a lot more to this specific admittance) this is just a synopsis. Through my experience, I have realised how God uses me to support others who are going through similar, serious or challenging situations which helps them to have some peace through the storm, in spite of how hard it may seem, which helps to fortify their faith.

I love Jesus, life, and anything aviation, nature, and outdoors.

My name is Evelyn Lamikanra. I remember how hurt I felt when my marriage packed up. I felt betrayed, that after making so much effort and giving so much

love, I was locked outside my home for another woman. Deprived of access to my children. After a while of bitterness and self-pity and weeping, I went to God in the place of prayer and fasting. I got an uplifting in my spirit and received a leading to give my love to others who need it.

That's how I adopted, my daughter Victoria. I transferred my little efforts into her upbringing and I got respite and peace in my spirit. This is me and Victoria on her graduation from Junior Secondary School. I adopted her, when she was only 5 years old. She's now 15years, and in Senior Secondary School. She's the only daughter of her family. All the others are boys. It was a journey, but the Lord saw me through it because he was always caring and carrying me in the hollow of his arms. To God be all the glory.

MOURN NO MORE
By Pastor Kemi Abidogun.
(General Overseer, Christ The Vine Church, Manchester and Bolton)

When you lose a loved one, people around you may not realise it, but you who have lost either your partner or child are actually mourning not for one, but for two people. This is because you not only lose your loved one....but you also lose yourself in the process of mourning as well.

When I lost my beloved husband in 2017, I went through the usual 6 processes of mourning, namely - shock, denial, anger, pain, acceptance and recovery.

In fact I don't think I have completed the process of recovery yet

Why? Because anytime I think of him, which is frequent, I still feel a hint of 'sadness' in my heart mixed with 'joy' from so many good memories of him as well. So, it's a mixed feeling.

Nevertheless, I am in a good place now - 7 years on, because my Abba Father, who is my Comforter, did an excellent job of bringing me through it all.

Today, I encourage my fellow women who are in mourning or who recently lost a loved one to LEAN on Jesus - our Sustainer, Protector, Hiding place, when the going gets tough.

The Bible says " weeping may endure for the night, but joy comes in the morning" (Psalm 30:5). So, no matter how tough it becomes, know that God will bring you through the flood of life.

In fact, you will be surprised to know that while you are going through the 6 stages of the mourning process, God is already carrying you and healing your spirit, soul and body day by day. It is during these periods that he will bring you old and new friends, helpers of destiny, divine assignments for you to do, even your tough experience can become the foundation for a new ministry to support others in the world.

So, I celebrate all the brave women out there who have once loved and lost someone; and today are embracing life with a SMILE on their faces having come out STRONGER through their experiences to become a TESTIMONY of God's goodness to mankind.

May God's Love, Joy and Peace abide with you for ever. Keep matching forward in life. You are never alone and you are doing great. God bless you. Amen.

I Believe

I believe in *Jesus Christ*; I believe that HE is the *only* Begotten Son of the Living God

I believe that He Is the Messiah, the <u>*only ONE*</u> who Liberates the oppressed

I believe that He was crucified for my sins on the cross of Calvary

I believe that He died, was buried and on the third day, He rose again from the grave -

As The Conquering Lion of the Tribe of Judah

I believe that He shall come again in His *glory!*

I believe in the resurrection of the saints in Christ

I believe that the trumpet shall sound and the dead in Christ shall arise first -

I believe that I shall behold Him, Face to Face. I believe that I shall behold the glory of the Son of God.

I am healed, I am saved, I am liberated (set free) by the Blood of Christ. Amen

Printed in Great Britain
by Amazon